·*Cooking for Today*·

THAI SIDE DISHES

THAI SIDE DISHES

SUE ASHWORTH

SIENA

A Siena Book
Siena is an imprint of Parragon Books

First published in Great Britain in 1996 by
Parragon Book Service Ltd
Unit 13–17
Avonbridge Trading Estate
Atlantic Road
Avonmouth
Bristol BS11 9QD

ISBN 0-7525-1500-4

Produced by Haldane Mason, London

Printed in Italy

Acknowledgements:
Art Direction: Ron Samuels
Editor: Joanna Swinnerton
Series Design: Pedro & Frances Prá-Lopez/Kingfisher Design
Page Design: Somewhere Creative
Photography: Iain Bagwell
Styling: Rachel Jukes
Home Economist: Sue Ashworth

Photographs on pages 6, 20, 36, 48 & 64 reproduced by permission of
ZEFA Picture Library (UK) Ltd

Note:
Cup measurements in this book are for American cups. Tablespoons are assumed to be 15 ml.
Unless otherwise stated, milk is assumed to be full-fat, eggs are standard size 2
and pepper is freshly ground black pepper.

Contents

CHAPTER ONE

Rice & Noodles

Rice and noodles form the backbone of Thai cookery and are usually the main component of the central dish, as well as appearing in side dishes and sometimes soups. Experiment with the recipes in this chapter to get a taste of the many ways in which rice and noodles feature in this imaginative and colourful cuisine.

Rice can make an appearance at the Thai table as a simple, plainly cooked side dish, or it can be a marvellous mixture of colours and flavours, full of surprises to the palate. Just try the recipe for Chilli Fried Rice to give a glorious example. 'Sticky' or glutinous rice is a mainstay in Thailand too, where it is used in desserts. One of the most popular snacks is Mangoes with Sticky Rice – served in banana leaves as a convenient and natural form of wrapping.

Noodles tend to be used in stir-fries in Thailand. In this chapter you will find two typical recipes for noodles, in which everything is quickly cooked in a wok or frying pan (skillet) to retain all the colour, flavour and goodness of the ingredients.

Look out for different varieties of rice and noodles in your supermarket – you'll be surprised at the range on display. And if you get the chance, visit a supplier of oriental foods to stock up your store cupboard with some of the more unusual types.

Opposite: *A small village in the hills of Thailand, not far from Chiang Mai.*

STEP 1

STEP 2

STEP 3

STEP 4

CRISPY NOODLES WITH CORIANDER (CILANTRO) & CUCUMBER

These crispy noodles will add a delicious crunch to your Thai meal.

SERVES 4

250 g/8 oz rice noodles
oil for deep-frying
2 garlic cloves, chopped finely
8 spring onions (scallions), trimmed and
  chopped finely
1 small red or green chilli, deseeded and
  chopped finely
2 tbsp fish sauce
2 tbsp light soy sauce
2 tbsp lime or lemon juice
2 tbsp molasses sugar

TO GARNISH:
spring onions (scallions), shredded
cucumber, sliced thinly
fresh chillies
fresh coriander (cilantro)

1 Break the noodles into smaller pieces with your hands.

2 Heat the oil for deep-frying in a wok or large frying pan (skillet). Add small batches of the noodles and fry them until pale golden brown and puffed up. Make sure that the oil is hot enough, or they will be tough. As each batch cooks, lift the noodles out with a perforated spoon on to paper towels.

3 When all the noodles are cooked, carefully pour off the oil into a separate container, then return 3 tablespoons of it to the wok or frying pan (skillet). Add the garlic, spring onions (scallions) and chilli, and stir-fry for about 2 minutes.

4 Mix together the fish sauce, soy sauce, lime or lemon juice and sugar. Add to the wok or frying pan (skillet) and cook for about 2 minutes, until the sugar has dissolved. Tip all the noodles back into the wok or frying pan (skillet) and toss lightly to coat with the sauce mixture. Avoid breaking them up too much.

5 Serve the noodles garnished with shredded spring onions (scallions), thinly sliced cucumber, chillies and fresh coriander (cilantro).

VARIATION

Stir-fry some uncooked peeled prawns (shrimp) or chopped raw chicken with the spring onions (scallions) and garlic in step 3. Cook for an extra 3–4 minutes to make sure they are thoroughly cooked.

STEP 1

STEP 2

STEP 3

STEP 4

SPICY CHICKEN & NOODLE SALAD

Strips of lean chicken are coated in a delicious spicy mixture, then stir-fried with noodles and served on a bed of salad in this quick and easy recipe.

SERVES 4

1 tsp finely grated fresh ginger root
½ tsp Chinese five-spice powder
1 tbsp plain (all-purpose) flour
½ tsp chilli powder
350 g/12 oz boned chicken breast, skinned and sliced thinly
60 g/2 oz rice noodles
125 g/4 oz/1½ cups Chinese leaves or hard white cabbage, shredded finely
7 cm/3 inch piece of cucumber, sliced finely
1 large carrot, pared thinly
1 tbsp olive oil
2 tbsp lime or lemon juice
2 tbsp sesame oil
salt and pepper

TO GARNISH:
lemon or lime slices
fresh coriander (cilantro) leaves

1 Mix together the ginger, five-spice powder, flour and chilli powder in a shallow mixing bowl. Season with salt and pepper. Add the strips of chicken and roll in the mixture until well coated.

2 Put the noodles into a large bowl and cover with warm water. Leave them to soak for about 5 minutes, then drain them well.

3 Mix together the Chinese leaves or cabbage, cucumber and carrot, and arrange them in a salad bowl. Whisk together the olive oil and lime or lemon juice, season with a little salt and pepper, and use to dress the salad.

4 Heat the sesame oil in a wok or frying pan (skillet) and add the chicken. Stir-fry for 5–6 minutes until well-browned and crispy on the outside. Remove from the wok or frying pan (skillet) with a perforated spoon and drain on paper towels.

5 Add the noodles to the wok or frying pan (skillet) and stir-fry for 3–4 minutes until heated through. Mix with the chicken and pile on top of the salad. Serve garnished with lime or lemon slices and coriander (cilantro) leaves.

TIPS

The easiest way to pare the carrot into fine strips is to use a potato peeler.
A few peanuts or cashew nuts, quickly stir-fried in a little sesame oil, add extra crunch and flavour to this salad.

STEP 1

STEP 2

STEP 3

STEP 4

CELLOPHANE NOODLES WITH SHRIMPS & BEAN-SPROUTS

Cellophane or 'glass' noodles are made from mung beans. They are sold dried, so they need soaking before use.

SERVES 4

2 tbsp light soy sauce
1 tbsp lime or lemon juice
1 tbsp fish sauce
125 g/4 oz firm tofu (bean curd), cut into chunks
125 g/4 oz cellophane noodles
2 tbsp sesame oil
4 shallots, sliced finely
2 garlic cloves, crushed
1 small red chilli, deseeded and chopped finely
2 celery sticks, sliced finely
2 carrots, sliced finely
125 g/4 oz/²/₃ cup cooked, peeled (small) shrimps
60 g/2 oz/1 cup bean-sprouts

TO GARNISH:
carrot slices
celery leaves
fresh chillies

1 Mix together the soy sauce, lime or lemon juice and fish sauce in a shallow bowl. Add the tofu (bean curd) cubes and toss them in the mixture. Cover and set aside for 15 minutes.

2 Put the noodles into a large bowl and cover with warm water. Leave them to soak for about 5 minutes, and then drain them well.

3 Heat the sesame oil in a wok or large frying pan (skillet). Add the shallots, garlic and chilli, and stir-fry for 1 minute. Add the celery and carrots, and stir-fry for a further 2–3 minutes.

4 Tip the drained noodles into the wok or frying pan (skillet) and cook, stirring, for 2 minutes, then add the shrimps, bean-sprouts and tofu (bean curd), with the soy sauce mixture. Cook over a medium high heat for 2–3 minutes until heated through.

5 Transfer to a serving dish and garnish with carrot slices, celery leaves and chillies.

SHRIMPS

For speed and convenience, use canned shrimps, but make sure that you drain them well first.

CHILLI FRIED RICE

Not so much a side dish as a meal in itself, this delicious fried rice can be served on its own or as an accompaniment to many Thai dishes.

STEP 1

SERVES 4

250 g/8 oz/generous 1 cup long-grain rice
4 tbsp vegetable oil
2 garlic cloves, chopped finely
1 small red chilli, deseeded and chopped finely
8 spring onions (scallions), trimmed and sliced finely
1 tbsp Thai red curry paste or 2 tsp chilli sauce
1 red (bell) pepper, cored, deseeded and chopped
90 g/ 3 oz/ ³/₄ cup dwarf green beans, chopped
250 g/8 oz/ 1¹/₂ cups cooked peeled prawns (shrimp) or chopped cooked chicken
2 tbsp fish sauce

TO GARNISH:
cucumber slices
shredded spring onion (scallion)

1 Cook the rice in plenty of boiling, lightly salted water until tender, about 12 minutes. Drain, rinse with cold water and drain thoroughly.

2 Heat the vegetable oil in a wok or large frying pan (skillet) and add the garlic. Fry gently for 2 minutes until golden. Add the chilli and spring onions (scallions) and cook, stirring, for 3–4 minutes.

3 Add the Thai curry paste or chilli sauce to the wok or frying pan (skillet) and fry for 1 minute, then add the red (bell) pepper and green beans. Stir-fry briskly for 2 minutes.

4 Tip the cooked rice into the wok or frying pan (skillet) and add the prawns (shrimp) or chicken. Stir-fry over a medium-high heat for about 4–5 minutes, until the rice is hot.

5 Serve garnished with cucumber slices and shredded spring onion (scallion).

STEP 2

STEP 3

RICE

Cook the rice the day before if you can remember – it will give an even better result. Alternatively, use rice left over from another dish to make this recipe.

Remember to cool any leftover rice quickly, then cover and refrigerate – it looks very innocent, but can be a cause of food poisoning if left out for any length of time in a warm environment.

STEP 4

STEP 2

STEP 3

STEP 4

STEP 5

STIR-FRIED NOODLES WITH THAI HOT SAUCE

This dish, like many Thai recipes, is very quick and simple to make. All the ingredients are cooked together in a wok, so there's very little washing-up to do!

SERVES 4

125 g/4 oz rice noodles
2 tbsp sesame oil
1 large garlic clove, crushed
125 g/4 oz pork fillet (tenderloin), sliced
    into strips
125 g/4 oz /²/₃ cup large prawns (shrimp),
    peeled and deveined
15 g/¹/₂ oz/1 tbsp dried shrimp (optional)
60 g/2 oz /¹/₂ cup white radish (mooli),
    grated
2 tbsp fish sauce
2 tbsp dark muscovado sugar
2 tbsp lime or lemon juice
60 g/2 oz/1 cup bean-sprouts
30 g/1 oz/¹/₄ cup peanuts, chopped
3–4 tbsp Thai hot sauce to serve

TO GARNISH:
2 shallots, sliced
fresh coriander (cilantro) leaves

1 Put the noodles into a large bowl and cover them with just-boiled water. Leave to soak for 15 minutes.

2 Heat the oil in a wok or large frying pan (skillet) and add the garlic, stir-frying for 2 minutes until golden brown. Add the strips of pork and stir-fry for a further 4–5 minutes.

3 Add the prawns (shrimp), dried shrimp (if using) and white radish (mooli) to the wok or frying pan (skillet) and stir-fry briskly for 2 minutes.

4 Stir in the fish sauce, sugar and lime or lemon juice.

5 Drain the noodles well and stir into the wok or frying pan (skillet) with the bean-sprouts and peanuts. Cook for 2–3 minutes, then serve.

6 Drizzle the Thai hot sauce over the noodles and garnish with the sliced shallot and coriander (cilantro) leaves.

VARIATIONS

If you have a good local supplier of oriental foods, buy some pickled white radish and use it instead of fresh. About 2 tablespoons will be enough.

Vary this recipe to suit your taste – the only rule is that there are no rules! Chicken makes a good alternative to pork, and if you love hot food, add 1–2 chopped fresh chillies. Chilli sauce can be used in place of the Thai hot sauce.

STEP 1

STEP 2

STEP 3

STEP 4

MANGOES WITH STICKY RICE

This traditional South-east Asian dessert has to be included in this book, as every Thai cook knows how to make it, and it will round off any Thai meal perfectly.

SERVES 4

125 g/4 oz/generous ½ cup glutinous
  (sticky) rice
250 ml/8 fl oz/1 cup coconut milk
60 g/2 oz/⅓ cup light muscovado sugar
½ tsp salt
1 tsp sesame seeds, toasted
4 ripe mangoes, peeled, halved, stoned
  (pitted) and sliced

1 Put the rice into a colander and rinse well with plenty of cold water until the water runs clear. Transfer the rice to a large bowl, cover with cold water and leave to soak overnight, or for at least 12 hours. Drain well.

2 Line a bamboo basket or steamer with muslin (cheesecloth) or finely woven cotton cloth. Add the rice and steam over a pan of gently simmering water until the rice is tender, about 40 minutes. Remove from the heat and transfer the rice to a bowl.

3 Reserve 4 tablespoons of the coconut milk and put the remainder into a small saucepan with the sugar and salt. Heat and simmer gently for about 8 minutes until reduced by about one third.

4 Pour the coconut milk mixture over the rice, fluffing up the rice so that the mixture is absorbed. Set aside for 10–15 minutes.

5 Pack the rice into individual moulds and then invert them on to serving plates. Pour a little reserved coconut milk over each mound and sprinkle with the sesame seeds. Arrange the sliced mango on the plates and serve, decorated with pieces of mango cut into shapes with tiny cutters.

STICKY RICE

Glutinous or sticky rice is available from stockists of Thai ingredients, although you can try making this recipe with short-grain pudding rice instead.

COCONUT MILK

Canned coconut milk is widely available from supermarkets, or you can buy packets of coconut cream, which can be mixed with milk or water to make coconut milk. Dried coconut milk, which can be reconstituted with water, is also available.

CHAPTER TWO

Fish & Seafood

Thousands of miles of coastline surround Thailand, and the country has many inland rivers and waterways, so it comes as no surprise to know that fish and seafood are extremely popular in Thai cookery. Being so cheap and plentiful, they are the main source of protein in the Thai diet. There is an amazing variety of fish and seafood constantly available, and no shortage of wonderful ways in which to cook it.

This chapter offers a tiny handful of recipes that use fish and seafood in side dishes – a taster of some of the best ways to sample some of Thailand's favourite food. Try, for example, the tasty Crab-meat Cakes, the King Prawns (Jumbo Shrimp) in Red Curry Sauce, or the Kaffir Lime Mussels with Lemon Grass.

When choosing fresh fish and seafood, always make sure that you buy from a reputable supermarket or fishmonger. Ask for advice when making your choice – if the fishmonger knows his or her business well, he or she will be able to help you. And don't forget to ask for help in preparing the catch. An expert fishmonger will deal with a pound or two of fresh squid far quicker than you can!

Opposite: *Thai fishermen sell their wares straight from the boat at a floating market in Saduak.*

STEP 1

STEP 2

STEP 3

STEP 5

PRAWNS (SHRIMP) WITH HOT & SWEET DIPPING SAUCE

Uncooked or 'green' prawns (shrimp) are speared on wooden skewers, brushed with a sesame oil, lime juice and fresh coriander (cilantro) baste, then grilled (broiled) until cooked. Enjoy their succulent flavour!

SERVES 4

wooden skewers soaked in warm water for 20 minutes
500 g/ 1 lb/ 2½ cups uncooked prawns (shrimp)
3 tbsp sesame oil
2 tbsp lime juice
1 tbsp chopped fresh coriander (cilantro)
sprigs of fresh coriander (cilantro) to garnish

SAUCE:
4 tbsp light malt vinegar
2 tbsp Thai fish sauce or light soy sauce
2 tbsp water
2 tbsp light muscovado sugar
2 garlic cloves, crushed
2 tsp grated fresh ginger root
1 red chilli, deseeded and chopped finely
2 tbsp chopped fresh coriander (cilantro)
salt

1 Peel the prawns (shrimp), leaving the tails intact. Remove the black vein that runs along the back of each one, then skewer the prawns (shrimp) on to the wooden skewers.

2 Mix together the sesame oil, lime juice and chopped coriander (cilantro) in a shallow bowl. Lay the skewered prawns (shrimp) in this mixture. Cover and chill for 30 minutes, turning once, so that the prawns (shrimp) absorb the marinade.

3 Meanwhile, make the sauce. Heat the vinegar, fish sauce or soy sauce, water, sugar and salt until boiling. Remove from the heat and leave to cool.

4 Mix together the garlic, ginger, chilli and coriander (cilantro) in a small serving bowl. Add the cooled vinegar mixture and stir together.

5 Place the prawns (shrimp) on a foil-lined grill (broiler) pan under a preheated grill (broiler) for about 6 minutes, turning once and basting often with the marinade, until cooked. Transfer to a warmed serving platter. Garnish with coriander (cilantro) and serve with the dipping sauce.

FRESH FISH

You can substitute firm fish for the prawns (shrimp) in this recipe if you wish. Fresh tuna or monkfish would be ideal. Just make sure that the fish is cooked through before you serve it.

STEP 1

STEP 2

STEP 3

STEP 4

KING PRAWNS (JUMBO SHRIMP) IN RED CURRY SAUCE

For something very quick and simple that sets your tastebuds alight, try this inspired dish of prawns (shrimp) in a wonderfully spicy sauce.

SERVES 4

1 tbsp vegetable oil
6 spring onions (scallions), trimmed and
   sliced
1 stalk lemon grass
1 cm/½ inch piece of fresh ginger root
250 ml/8 fl oz/1 cup coconut milk
2 tbsp Thai red curry paste
1 tbsp fish sauce
500 g/1 lb/3 cups uncooked king prawns
   (jumbo shrimp)
1 tbsp chopped fresh coriander (cilantro)
fresh chillies to garnish

1 Heat the vegetable oil in a wok or large frying pan (skillet) and fry the spring onions (scallions) gently until softened, about 2 minutes.

2 Bruise the stalk of lemon grass using a meat mallet or rolling pin. Peel and finely grate the piece of fresh ginger root.

3 Add the bruised lemon grass and grated ginger root to the wok or frying pan (skillet) with the coconut milk, Thai red curry paste and fish sauce. Heat until almost boiling.

4 Peel the prawns (shrimp), leaving the tails intact. Remove the black vein running down the back of each prawn (shrimp). Add the prawns (shrimp) to the wok or frying pan (skillet) with the chopped coriander (cilantro) and cook gently for 5 minutes.

5 Serve the prawns (shrimp) with the sauce, garnished with fresh chillies.

VARIATIONS

Try this recipe using Thai green curry sauce instead of red. Both varieties are obtainable from many supermarkets – look for them in the oriental foods section.

Use 3 shallots or ½ small onion instead of the spring onions (scallions), if you prefer.

STEP 1

STEP 2

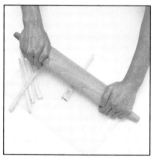

STEP 3

STEP 4

KAFFIR LIME MUSSELS WITH LEMON GRASS

Give fresh mussels a Far Eastern flavour by using some Kaffir lime leaves, garlic and lemon grass in the stock used for steaming them.

SERVES 4

750 g/ 1 ½ lb live mussels
1 tbsp sesame oil
3 shallots, chopped finely
2 garlic cloves, chopped finely
1 stalk lemon grass
2 Kaffir lime leaves
2 tbsp chopped fresh coriander (cilantro)
finely grated rind of 1 lime
2 tbsp lime juice
300 ml/ ½ pint/ 1 ¼ cups hot vegetable stock
crusty bread to serve

TO GARNISH:
sprigs of fresh coriander (cilantro)
lime wedges

1 Using a small sharp knife, scrape the beards off the mussels under cold running water. Scrub them well, discarding any that are damaged or remain open when tapped. Keep rinsing until there is no trace of sand.

2 Heat the sesame oil in a large saucepan and fry the shallots and garlic gently until softened, about 2 minutes.

3 Bruise the lemon grass, using a meat mallet or rolling pin.

4 Add the lemon grass to the saucepan with the Kaffir lime leaves, coriander (cilantro), lime rind and juice, mussels and stock. Put the lid on the saucepan and cook over a moderate heat so that the mussels steam for 3–5 minutes. Shake the saucepan from time to time.

5 Check that the mussels have opened and discard any that remain shut. Lift them out into 4 warmed soup plates. Boil the remaining liquid rapidly so that it reduces slightly. Remove the lemon grass and Kaffir lime leaves, then pour the liquid over the mussels.

6 Garnish with the fresh coriander (cilantro) and lime wedges, and serve at once with chunks of crusty bread to soak up the juices.

MUSSELS

Mussels are now farmed, so they should be available from good fishmongers throughout the year.

STEP 1

STEP 2

STEP 3

STEP 4

SHRIMP ROLLS

This variation of a spring roll is made with shrimps, stir-fried with shallots, carrot, cucumber, bamboo shoots and rice.

SERVES 4

2 tbsp vegetable oil
3 shallots, chopped very finely
1 carrot, cut into matchstick pieces
7 cm/ 3 inch piece of cucumber, cut into matchstick pieces
60 g/ 2 oz/¹/₂ cup bamboo shoots, shredded finely
125 g/ 4 oz/¹/₂ cup peeled (small) shrimps
90 g/ 3 oz/¹/₂ cup cooked long-grain rice
1 tbsp fish sauce or light soy sauce
1 tsp sugar
2 tsp cornflour (cornstarch), blended in 2 tbsp cold water
8 × 25 cm/ 10 inch spring roll wrappers
oil for deep-frying
salt and pepper
Thai plum sauce to serve

TO GARNISH:
spring onion (scallion) brushes (see page 34)
sprigs of fresh coriander (cilantro)

1 Heat the oil in a wok or frying pan (skillet) and add the shallots, carrot, cucumber and bamboo shoots. Stir-fry briskly for 2–3 minutes. Add the shrimps and cooked rice, and cook for a further 2 minutes. Season.

2 Mix together the fish sauce or soy sauce, sugar and blended cornflour (cornstarch). Add to the stir-fry and cook, stirring constantly, for about 1 minute, until thickened. Leave to cool slightly.

3 Place spoonfuls of the shrimp and vegetable mixture on the spring roll wrappers. Dampen the edges and roll them up to enclose the filling completely.

4 Heat the oil for deep-frying and fry the spring rolls until crisp and golden brown. Drain on paper towels.

5 Serve the shrimp rolls garnished with spring onion (scallion) brushes and fresh coriander (cilantro) and accompanied by the plum sauce.

TIPS

Keep the unfilled spring roll wrappers covered with a clean, damp cloth as you work to prevent them from drying out. Follow the wrapping instructions carefully so that the filling is properly enclosed.
You need 30 g/1 oz/2 tablespoons long-grain rice to give 90 g/3 oz/¹/₂ cup cooked rice.

THAI-STYLE SEAFOOD OMELETTE

This delicious omelette is filled with a mixture of fresh vegetables, sliced squid and prawns (shrimp).

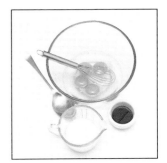

STEP 1

SERVES 4

4 eggs
3 tbsp milk
1 tbsp fish sauce or light soy sauce
1 tbsp sesame oil
3 shallots, sliced finely
1 small red (bell) pepper, cored, deseeded and
  sliced very finely
1 small leek, trimmed and cut into
  matchstick pieces
125 g/4 oz squid rings
125 g/4 oz/²⁄₃ cup cooked peeled prawns
  (shrimp)
1 tbsp chopped fresh basil
15 g/¹⁄₂ oz/1 tbsp butter
salt and pepper
sprigs of fresh basil to garnish

1 Beat the eggs, milk and fish sauce or soy sauce together.

2 Heat the sesame oil in a wok or large frying pan (skillet) and add all the vegetables. Stir-fry briskly for 2–3 minutes.

3 Add the squid, prawns (shrimp) and chopped basil to the wok or frying pan (skillet). Stir-fry for a further 2–3 minutes, until the squid looks opaque. Season with salt and pepper.

Transfer to a warmed plate and keep warm.

4 Melt the butter in a large omelette pan or frying pan (skillet) and add the beaten egg mixture. Cook over a medium-high heat until just set.

5 Spoon the vegetable and seafood mixture in a line down the middle of the omelette, then fold each side of the omelette over. Transfer to a warmed serving dish and cut into 4 portions. Garnish with sprigs of fresh basil and serve at once.

STEP 2

STEP 3

STEP 5

VARIATIONS

Chopped, cooked chicken makes a delicious alternative to the squid.
  Use fresh coriander (cilantro) instead of the basil for a change.

STEP 2

STEP 3

STEP 4

STEP 5

CRAB-MEAT CAKES

Make these tasty crab-meat cakes, with their flavour of Thailand, to serve as a snack or starter, or as an accompaniment to a main meal.

SERVES 4

90 g/ 3 oz/generous 1 cup long-grain rice
1 tbsp sesame oil
1 small onion, chopped finely
1 large garlic clove, crushed
2 tbsp chopped fresh coriander (cilantro)
200 g/7 oz can of crab meat, drained
1 tbsp fish sauce or light soy sauce
250 ml/8 fl oz/1 cup coconut milk
2 eggs
4 tbsp vegetable oil
salt and pepper
sliced spring onions (scallions), to garnish

1 Cook the rice in plenty of boiling, lightly salted water until just tender, about 12 minutes. Rinse with cold water and drain well.

2 Heat the sesame oil in a small frying pan (skillet) and fry the onion and garlic gently for about 5 minutes, until softened and golden brown.

3 In a large bowl, mix together the rice, onion, garlic, coriander (cilantro), crab meat, fish sauce or soy sauce and coconut milk. Season with salt and pepper. Beat the eggs together and add to the mixture.

4 Divide the mixture between 8 greased ramekin dishes or teacups and place them in a baking dish or roasting tin (pan) with enough warm water to come halfway up their sides. Place in a preheated oven at 180°C/ 350°F/Gas Mark 4 for about 25 minutes, until set. Leave to cool.

5 Turn the crab cakes out of the ramekin dishes or teacups. Heat the vegetable oil in a wok or frying pan (skillet) and fry the crab cakes in the oil until golden brown. Drain on paper towels and serve at once, garnished with sliced spring onions (scallions).

PREPARING AHEAD

If you want, you can prepare these crab cakes up to the point where they have been baked. Cool them, then cover and chill, ready for frying when needed.

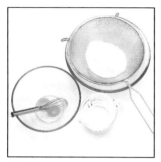

STEP 1

STEP 2

STEP 3

STEP 4

SHRIMP & SWEETCORN PATTIES

Chopped shrimps and sweetcorn are combined in a light batter, which is dropped in spoonfuls into hot fat to make these tasty patties.

SERVES 4

125 g/4 oz/1 cup plain (all-purpose) flour
1½ tsp baking powder
½ tsp salt
2 eggs
about 250 ml/8 fl oz/1 cup cold water
1 garlic clove, very finely chopped
3 spring onions (scallions), trimmed and
    very finely chopped
250 g/8 oz/1 cup peeled (small) shrimps,
    chopped
125 g/4 oz/½ cup canned sweetcorn,
    drained
vegetable oil for frying
pepper

TO GARNISH:
spring onion (scallion) brushes
lime slices
1 chilli flower (see page 68)

1 Sift the flour, baking powder and salt into a large bowl. Add the eggs and half the water. Use a whisk to beat the mixture together to make a smooth batter, adding extra water to give the consistency of double (heavy) cream.

2 Add the garlic and spring onions (scallions) to the batter. Cover and set aside for about 30 minutes.

3 Stir the shrimps and sweetcorn into the batter, mixing well. Season with pepper.

4 Heat 2–3 tablespoons of vegetable oil in a frying pan (skillet). Drop tablespoonfuls of the batter into the pan and cook over a medium heat until bubbles rise and the surface just sets. Flip the patties over and cook the other side until golden brown. Drain on paper towels.

5 Cook the remaining batter in the same way, adding more vegetable oil to the frying pan (skillet) as required.

6 Garnish with a spring onion (scallion) brush, lime slices and a chilli flower and serve at once.

SPRING ONION (SCALLION) BRUSHES

Make a spring onion (scallion) brush by trimming off the tips of the leaves and making several fine cuts from the leaf tips to the top of the bulb. Place in iced water to make the leaves curl.

34

CHAPTER THREE

Poultry Dishes

Chicken is a very popular choice for Thai recipes, as its versatile flavour marries so well with other ingredients. It is inexpensive too, which is a bonus. Other poultry, such as duck, is also used, though less frequently as it tends to be more expensive; it is often saved for special occasions.

In most recipes the meat is shredded, chopped or finely minced (ground), so that it combines well with other ingredients and also cooks quickly – especially important for stir-fries and grilled (broiled) or barbecued dishes. Try Sesame Skewered Chicken with Ginger Baste, where the chicken is marinated in a delicious spicy mixture, then threaded on to wooden satay sticks and cooked until golden. And savour the lively flavours in Lime & Coriander (Cilantro) Chicken Fried Rice – if you enjoy it as a side dish, try it as a main course another time.

If you are planning a meal for a large number of guests, make sure that you get the preparations well in hand before their arrival. It's a good idea to measure and assemble all the ingredients that go in any one dish on a large plate, so that you are ready to proceed with the cooking when thc time is right. And because Thai cooking is so quick, you'll have time to enjoy the company of your guests!

Opposite: *An exotic Thai temple is reflected in the waters at Mae Hong Son.*

THAI CHICKEN SPRING ROLLS

A cucumber dipping sauce tastes perfect with these delicious spring rolls, filled with chicken and fresh, crunchy vegetables.

STEP 1

STEP 2

STEP 3

STEP 4

SERVES 4

2 tbsp vegetable oil
4 spring onions (scallions), trimmed and
    sliced very finely
1 carrot, cut into matchstick pieces
1 small green or red (bell) pepper, cored,
    deseeded and sliced finely
60 g/2 oz/²/₃ cup button mushrooms, sliced
60 g/2 oz/1 cup bean-sprouts
175 g/6 oz/1 cup cooked chicken, shredded
1 tbsp light soy sauce
1 tsp sugar
2 tsp cornflour (cornstarch), blended in 2
    tbsp cold water
12 × 20 cm/8 inch spring roll wrappers
oil for deep-frying
salt and pepper
spring onion (scallion) brushes to garnish
    (see page 34)

SAUCE:
50 ml/2 fl oz/¹/₄ cup light malt vinegar
2 tbsp water
60 g/2 oz/¹/₄ cup light muscovado sugar
¹/₂ tsp salt
5 cm/2 inch piece of cucumber, peeled and
    chopped finely
4 spring onions (scallions), trimmed and
    sliced finely
1 small red or green chilli, deseeded and
    chopped very finely

1 Heat the oil in a wok or frying pan (skillet) and add the spring onions (scallions), carrot and (bell) pepper. Stir-fry for 2–3 minutes. Add the mushrooms, bean-sprouts and chicken and cook for a further 2 minutes. Season to taste.

2 Mix together the soy sauce, sugar and blended cornflour (cornstarch). Add to the stir-fry and cook, stirring continuously for about 1 minute, until thickened. Leave to cool slightly.

3 Place spoonfuls of the chicken and vegetable mixture on the spring roll wrappers. Dampen the edges and roll them up to enclose the filling completely.

4 To make the dipping sauce, heat the vinegar, water, sugar and salt in a saucepan. Boil for 1 minute. Mix the cucumber, spring onions (scallions) and chilli in a small serving bowl and pour over the vinegar mixture. Leave to cool.

5 Heat the oil and fry the rolls until crisp and golden brown. Drain on paper towels, then serve, garnished with spring onion (scallion) brushes and accompanied by the cucumber dipping sauce.

STEP 1

STEP 2

STEP 3

STEP 4

SESAME SKEWERED CHICKEN WITH GINGER BASTE

Chunks of chicken breast are marinated in a mixture of lime juice, garlic, sesame oil and fresh ginger to give them a great flavour.

SERVES 4

4 wooden satay sticks, soaked in warm
　water
500 g/1 lb boneless chicken breasts
sprigs of fresh mint to garnish

MARINADE:
1 garlic clove, crushed
1 shallot, chopped very finely
2 tbsp sesame oil
1 tbsp fish sauce or light soy sauce
finely grated rind of 1 lime or $\frac{1}{2}$ lemon
2 tbsp lime juice or lemon juice
1 tsp sesame seeds
2 tsp finely grated fresh ginger root
2 tsp chopped fresh mint
salt and pepper

1 To make the marinade, put the garlic, shallot, sesame oil, fish sauce or soy sauce, lime or lemon rind and juice, sesame seeds, ginger and chopped mint into a large non-metallic bowl. Season with a little salt and pepper.

2 Remove the skin from the chicken breasts and cut the flesh into chunks. Add them to the marinade, stirring to coat them in the mixture. Cover and chill for at least 2 hours so that the flavours are absorbed.

3 Thread the chicken on to wooden satay sticks. Place them on the rack of a grill (broiler) pan and baste with the marinade.

4 Place the kebabs under a preheated grill (broiler) for about 8–10 minutes. Turn them frequently, basting them with the remaining marinade.

5 Serve at once, garnished with sprigs of fresh mint.

V A R I A T I O N S

Pork fillet (tenderloin) or turkey breasts can be used instead of the chicken.
　The kebabs taste delicious if dipped into an accompanying bowl of hot chilli sauce.

STEP 1

STEP 2

STEP 3

STEP 4

CHICKEN & MUSHROOM WON-TONS

These deliciously crispy nibbles make an ideal introduction to a Thai meal. Here they are filled with a chicken and mushroom mixture.

SERVES 4

250 g/8 oz boneless chicken breast, skinned
60 g/2 oz/²⁄₃ cup mushrooms
1 garlic clove
2 shallots
1 tbsp fish sauce or mushroom ketchup
1 tbsp chopped fresh coriander (cilantro)
2 tbsp vegetable oil
about 50 won-ton wrappers
oil for deep-frying
salt and pepper
sliced spring onion (scallion) to garnish
sweet chilli sauce to serve

1 Put the chicken, mushrooms, garlic, shallots, fish sauce or mushroom ketchup and coriander (cilantro) into a blender or food processor. Blend for 10–15 seconds. Alternatively, chop all the ingredients finely and mix them together well.

2 Heat the vegetable oil in a wok or frying pan (skillet) and add the chicken mixture. Stir-fry for about 8 minutes, breaking up the mixture as it cooks, until it browns. Transfer to a bowl and leave to cool for 10–15 minutes.

3 Place the won-ton wrappers on a clean, damp tea towel (dish cloth).

Layering 2 wrappers together at a time, place teaspoonfuls of the chicken mixture into the middle. Dampen the edges with water, then make small pouches, pressing the edges together to seal. Repeat with the remaining wrappers until all the mixture is used.

4 Heat the oil in a wok or deep fat fryer. Fry the won-tons, a few at a time, for about 2–3 minutes until golden brown. Lift them from the oil with a perforated spoon and drain on paper towels. Keep warm while frying the remaining won-tons.

5 Transfer the won-tons to a warmed serving platter and garnish with sliced spring onion (scallion). Serve at once, accompanied by some sweet chilli sauce.

VARIATIONS

Use 125 g/4 oz/½ cup of peeled prawns (shrimp) mixed with 125 g/4 oz/½ cup lean minced (ground) pork to make a different variety, omitting the mushrooms.
If won-ton wrappers are unavailable, use sheets of filo pastry cut to size.

DUCKLING & RADISH SALAD

Juicy duckling breasts are coated with sesame seeds, then cooked, thinly sliced and served with a crisp salad.

STEP 1

STEP 2

STEP 3

STEP 4

SERVES 4

350 g/12 oz boneless duckling breasts, skinned
2 tbsp plain (all-purpose) flour
1 egg
2 tbsp water
2 tbsp sesame seeds
3 tbsp sesame oil
½ head of Chinese leaves, shredded
3 celery sticks, sliced finely
8 radishes, trimmed and halved
salt and pepper
fresh basil leaves to garnish

DRESSING:
finely grated rind of 1 lime
2 tbsp lime juice
2 tbsp olive oil
1 tbsp light soy sauce
1 tbsp chopped fresh basil

1 Put each duckling breast between sheets of greaseproof paper (baking parchment) or clingfilm (plastic wrap). Use a meat mallet or rolling pin to beat them out and flatten them slightly.

2 Sprinkle the flour on to a large plate and season with salt and pepper. Beat the egg and water together in a shallow bowl, then sprinkle the sesame seeds on to a separate plate. Dip the duckling breasts first into the seasoned flour, then into the egg mixture and finally into the sesame seeds.

3 Heat the sesame oil in a wok or frying pan (skillet) and fry the duckling breasts over a medium heat for about 8 minutes, turning once. Insert a sharp knife into the thickest part – the juices should run clear. Lift them out and drain on paper towels.

4 To make the dressing for the salad, whisk together the lime rind and juice, olive oil, soy sauce and chopped basil. Season with a little salt and pepper.

5 Arrange the Chinese leaves, celery and radish on a serving plate. Slice the duckling breasts thinly and place on top of the salad. Drizzle with the dressing and garnish with fresh basil leaves. Serve at once.

VARIATIONS

Use fresh coriander (cilantro) or mint as an alternative to basil.
Either chicken or turkey breasts would make excellent alternatives to duckling.

STEP 1

STEP 2

STEP 3

STEP 4

LIME & CORIANDER (CILANTRO) CHICKEN FRIED RICE

Lime rind and juice is combined with chopped fresh coriander (cilantro) to give this fried rice recipe a very lively flavour.

SERVES 4

250 g/8 oz/generous 1 cup long-grain rice
4 tbsp vegetable oil
2 garlic cloves, chopped finely
1 small green chilli, deseeded and chopped
  finely
5 shallots, sliced finely
1 tbsp Thai green curry paste
1 yellow or green (bell) pepper, cored,
  deseeded and chopped
2 celery sticks, sliced finely
250 g/8 oz/1½ cups cooked chicken,
  chopped
2 tbsp light soy sauce
finely grated rind of 1 lime
2 tbsp lime juice
1 tbsp chopped fresh coriander (cilantro)
30 g/1 oz/¼ cup unsalted peanuts, toasted

TO GARNISH:
fresh coriander (cilantro)
finely sliced shallots
lime slices

1 Cook the rice in plenty of boiling, lightly salted water until tender, about 12 minutes. Drain, rinse with cold water and drain thoroughly.

2 Heat the oil in a wok or large frying pan (skillet) and add the garlic. Fry gently for 2 minutes until golden. Add the chilli and shallots, and cook, stirring, for a further 3–4 minutes.

3 Add the Thai curry paste to the wok or frying pan (skillet) and fry for 1 minute, then add the yellow or green (bell) pepper and celery. Stir-fry briskly for 2 minutes.

4 Tip the cooked rice into the wok or frying pan (skillet) and add the chicken, soy sauce, lime rind and juice and chopped coriander (cilantro). Stir-fry over a medium-high heat for about 4–5 minutes, until the rice is hot.

5 Serve sprinkled with the peanuts and garnished with sprigs of fresh coriander (cilantro), sliced shallots and lime slices.

TIPS

If you don't have a lime handy, but you do have a lemon, use that instead – about half the juice will be enough.

The rice is best if it is cooked the day before. Cover it and keep it chilled until you need it.

CHAPTER FOUR

Beef & Pork

In Thai cookery meat is generally used for special occasions only, to mark a particular event with a celebration or a feast. Thailand is more of a seafood-eating nation than a meat-eating one, so meat is mainly used in small amounts to add flavour and variety to dishes, and is combined with lots of other ingredients to make it go further. Another factor is that in Thailand meat can be expensive, so it is used sparingly.

In this chapter you will find some delicious ideas, from the widely known Pork Satay with a simple-to-make spicy peanut sauce, to the more unusual 'Fat Horses' – a fascinating recipe for a mixture of minced (ground) pork, chicken and prawns (shrimp) combined with lots of exciting flavourings cooked together to make an enticing side dish. And if you've ever tried Pork & Prawn (Shrimp) Sesame Toasts in a Thai restaurant, you will be pleased to find this delicious recipe explained here.

The principle of using a little meat with plenty of vegetables, rice and noodles is very sound, nutritionally speaking. It means that our intake of important nutrients – such as vitamins, minerals and complex carbohydrates – is kept high, while our fat intake remains low. Fresh vegetables provide lots of fibre too – essential for keeping our bodies fit from the inside!

Opposite: *Kata Noi beach at dusk.*

STEP 1

STEP 2

STEP 3

STEP 4

PORK & PRAWN (SHRIMP) SESAME TOASTS

This classic Thai snack is a great nibble for serving at parties – but be sure to make plenty!

SERVES 4

250 g/8 oz lean pork
250 g/8 oz/²/₃ cup uncooked peeled prawns (shrimp), deveined
4 spring onions (scallions), trimmed
1 garlic clove, crushed
1 tbsp chopped fresh coriander (cilantro) leaves and stems
1 tbsp fish sauce
1 egg
8–10 slices of thick-cut white bread
3 tbsp sesame seeds
150 ml/¹/₄ pint/²/₃ cup vegetable oil
salt and pepper

TO GARNISH:
sprigs of fresh coriander (cilantro)
red (bell) pepper, sliced finely

1 Put the pork, prawns (shrimp), spring onions (scallions), garlic, coriander (cilantro), fish sauce, egg and seasoning into a food processor or blender. Process for a few seconds to chop the ingredients finely. Transfer the mixture to a bowl. Alternatively, chop the pork, prawns (shrimp) and spring onions (scallions) very finely, and mix with the garlic, coriander (cilantro), fish sauce, beaten egg and seasoning until well combined.

2 Spread the pork and prawn (shrimp) mixture thickly over the bread so that it reaches right up to the edges. Cut off the crusts and slice each piece of bread into 4 squares or triangles.

3 Sprinkle the topping liberally with sesame seeds.

4 Heat the oil in a wok or frying pan (skillet). Fry a few pieces of the bread, topping side down first so that it sets the egg, for about 2 minutes or until golden brown. Turn the pieces over to cook on the other side, about 1 minute.

5 Drain the pork and prawn (shrimp) toasts and place them on paper towels. Fry the remaining pieces in batches until they are all cooked.

6 Serve garnished with sprigs of fresh coriander (cilantro) and strips of red (bell) pepper.

PRAWNS (SHRIMP)

If you can't find any uncooked prawns (shrimp), use cooked ones instead. If using frozen prawns (shrimp), be sure to defrost them first and dry them with paper towels.

STEP 1

STEP 2

STEP 3

STEP 4

PORK SATAY

Small pieces of tender pork are skewered on bamboo satay sticks, grilled (broiled) or barbecued, then served with a delicious peanut sauce.

SERVES 4

8 bamboo satay sticks, soaked in warm
    water
500 g/1 lb pork fillet (tenderloin)

SAUCE:
125 g/4oz/1 cup unsalted peanuts
2 tsp hot chilli sauce
180 ml/6 fl oz/³/₄ cup coconut milk
2 tbsp soy sauce
1 tbsp ground coriander
pinch of ground turmeric
1 tbsp dark muscovado sugar
salt

TO GARNISH:
fresh flat leaf (Italian) parsley or coriander
    (cilantro)
cucumber leaves
red chillies

1 To make the sauce, scatter the peanuts on a baking (cookie) sheet and toast under a preheated grill (broiler) until golden brown, turning them once or twice. Leave to cool, then grind them in a food processor, blender or food mill. Alternatively, chop them very finely.

2 Put the ground peanuts into a small saucepan with all the remaining sauce ingredients. Heat gently, stirring constantly. Reduce the heat to very low and cook gently for 5 minutes.

3 Meanwhile, trim any fat from the pork. Cut the pork into small cubes and thread it on to the bamboo satay sticks. Place the kebabs on a rack covered with foil in a grill (broiler) pan.

4 Put half the peanut sauce into a small serving bowl. Brush the skewered pork with the remaining satay sauce and place under a preheated grill (broiler) for about 10 minutes, turning and basting frequently, until cooked.

5 Serve the pork with the reserved peanut sauce and garnish with flat leaf (Italian) parsley or coriander (cilantro) leaves, cucumber leaves and red chillies.

CUCUMBER LEAVES

To make cucumber leaves, slice a thick chunk from the side of a cucumber, and cut to shape. Cut grooves in the cucumber flesh in the shape of leaf veins.

STEP 1

STEP 2

STEP 3

STEP 4

FAT HORSES

The curious name for this traditional steamed or baked Thai dish conjures up quite a picture! It is a mixture of minced (ground) pork, chicken and crab meat, flavoured with coconut milk, fish sauce and coriander (cilantro).

SERVES 6

30 g/1 oz/2 tbsp creamed coconut
125 g/4 oz lean pork
125 g/4 oz chicken breast, skin removed
125 g/4 oz/¹/₂ cup canned crab meat, drained
2 eggs
2 garlic cloves, crushed
4 spring onions (scallions), trimmed and chopped
1 tbsp fish sauce
1 tbsp chopped fresh coriander (cilantro) leaves and stems
1 tbsp dark muscovado sugar
salt and pepper

TO GARNISH:
finely sliced white radish (mooli) or turnip
chives
red chilli
sprigs of fresh coriander (cilantro)

1 Put the coconut into a bowl and pour over 3 tablespoons of hot water. Stir to dissolve the coconut.

2 Put the pork, chicken and crab meat into a food processor or blender and process for 10–15 seconds until minced (ground), or chop them finely by hand and put in a mixing bowl.

3 Add the coconut mixture to the food processor or blender with the eggs, garlic, spring onions (scallions), fish sauce, coriander (cilantro) and sugar. Season with salt and pepper and process for a few more seconds. Alternatively, mix these ingredients into the chopped pork, chicken and crab meat.

4 Grease 6 ramekin dishes with a little butter. Spoon in the minced (ground) mixture, levelling the surface. Place them in a steamer, then set the steamer over a pan of gently boiling water. Cook until set – about 30 minutes.

5 Lift out the dishes and leave to cool for a few minutes. Run a knife around the edge of each dish, then invert on to warmed plates. Serve garnished with finely sliced white radish (mooli) or turnip, chives, red chilli and sprigs of fresh coriander (cilantro).

BAKING

You can bake the mixture in a preheated oven at 180°C/350°F/Gas Mark 4 for 30 minutes if preferred, placing the dishes in a roasting tin (pan), with enough warm water to come halfway up their sides.

MEATBALLS IN SPICY PEANUT SAUCE

Choose very lean minced (ground) beef to make these meatballs – or better still, buy some lean beef and mince (grind) it yourself.

STEP 1

SERVES 4

500 g/ 1 lb/ 2 cups lean minced (ground)
  beef
2 tsp finely grated fresh ginger root
1 small red chilli, deseeded and chopped
  finely
1 tbsp chopped fresh basil or coriander
  (cilantro)
1 tbsp sesame oil
1 tbsp vegetable oil
salt and pepper

SAUCE:
2 tbsp Thai red curry paste
300 ml/ ¹/₂ pint/ 1¹/₄ cups coconut milk
125 g/ 4 oz/ 1 cup ground peanuts
1 tbsp fish sauce

TO GARNISH:
chopped fresh basil
sprigs of fresh basil or coriander (cilantro)

1 Put the beef, ginger, chilli and basil or coriander (cilantro) into a food processor or blender. Add ¹/₂ teaspoon of salt and plenty of pepper. Process for about 10–15 seconds until finely chopped. Alternatively, chop the ingredients finely and mix together.

2 Form the beef mixture into about 12 balls. Heat the sesame oil and vegetable oil in a wok or frying pan (skillet) and fry the meatballs over a medium-high heat until well browned on all sides, about 10 minutes. Lift them out and drain on paper towels.

3 To make the sauce, stir-fry the red curry paste in the wok or frying pan (skillet) for 1 minute. Add the coconut milk, peanuts and fish sauce. Heat, stirring, until just simmering.

4 Return the meatballs to the wok or frying pan (skillet) and cook gently in the sauce for 10–15 minutes. If the sauce begins to get too thick, add a little extra coconut milk or water. Season with a little salt and pepper, if needed.

5 Serve garnished with chopped fresh basil and sprigs of fresh basil or coriander (cilantro).

ALTERNATIVE

Minced (ground) lamb makes a delicious alternative to beef. If you do use lamb, try substituting ground almonds for the peanuts and fresh mint for the basil.

STEP 2

STEP 3

STEP 4

STEP 1

STEP 2

STEP 3

STEP 4

ROAST RED PORK

Pork fillet (tenderloin) is given a marvellous flavour and distinctive red colour in this excellent recipe.

SERVES 4

750 g/1½ lb pork fillet (tenderloin)
1 tsp red food colouring
4 garlic cloves, crushed
1 tsp Chinese five-spice powder
1 tbsp light soy sauce
1 tbsp fish sauce
1 tbsp dry sherry
1 tbsp dark muscovado sugar
1 tbsp sesame oil
1 tbsp finely grated fresh ginger root

TO GARNISH:
lettuce
spring onions (scallions), finely sliced

1 Rinse the pork fillet (tenderloin) and trim off any fat. Place in a large clear plastic food bag or freezer bag and add the red food colouring. Roll the pork around in the bag to coat it in the colouring.

2 Mix all the remaining ingredients together in a bowl.

3 Add the mixture to the pork in the plastic bag. Secure the opening and chill overnight, or for at least 12 hours, turning the bag over occasionally.

4 Place the pork on a rack over a roasting tin (pan) and cook in a preheated oven at 220°C/425°F/Gas Mark 7 for 15 minutes. Remove from the oven and baste with the remaining marinade.

5 Reduce the oven temperature to 180°C/350°F/Gas Mark 4 and return the pork to the oven to roast for a further 25 minutes, basting occasionally with any remaining marinade. Leave to cool for at least 10 minutes before slicing.

6 Slice thinly, arrange on a serving platter and garnish with lettuce and finely sliced spring onions (scallions).

PORK

Putting the pork in a plastic bag helps to prevent your hands from turning red from the food colouring.

Roast red pork makes an excellent addition to stir-fries and fried rice and noodle dishes.

STEP 1

STEP 2

STEP 3

STEP 4

STIR-FRIED PORK & CABBAGE

Rustle up this quick-to-cook side dish in a matter of moments. Assemble all your ingredients first, then everything is ready to hand as you start to stir-fry.

SERVES 4

375 g/12 oz pork fillet (tenderloin)
8 spring onions (scallions), trimmed
½ small white cabbage
½ cucumber
2 tsp finely grated fresh ginger root
1 tbsp fish sauce or light soy sauce
2 tbsp dry sherry
2 tbsp water
2 tsp cornflour (cornstarch)
1 tbsp chopped fresh mint or coriander (cilantro)
2 tbsp sesame oil
salt and pepper

TO GARNISH:
sprigs of fresh mint or coriander (cilantro)
1 chilli flower (see page 68)

1 Slice the pork very thinly. Shred the spring onions (scallions) and cabbage, and cut the cucumber into matchstick strips.

2 Mix together the ginger, fish sauce or soy sauce, sherry, water, cornflour (cornstarch) and chopped mint or coriander (cilantro) until blended.

3 Heat the sesame oil in a wok or large frying pan (skillet) and add the pork. Stir-fry briskly over a high heat until browned, about 4–5 minutes.

4 Add the spring onions (scallions), cabbage and cucumber and stir-fry for a further 2 minutes. Add the blended cornflour (cornstarch) mixture and continue to cook for about 1 minute, until the pork and vegetables are coated with the mixture and it has thickened slightly. Season to taste with salt and pepper.

5 Transfer the stir-fry to a warmed dish and serve at once, garnished with sprigs of fresh mint or coriander (cilantro) and a chilli flower.

ROAST RED PORK

Roast Red Pork is excellent used in this stir-fry, as it adds both extra colour and flavour. See the recipe on page 58.

STEP 1

STEP 2

STEP 3

STEP 4

THAI STUFFED COURGETTES (ZUCCHINI)

Hollow out some courgettes (zucchini), fill them with a spicy beef mixture and bake them in the oven for a delicious side dish.

SERVES 4

8 medium courgettes (zucchini)
1 tbsp sesame or vegetable oil
1 garlic clove, crushed
2 shallots, chopped finely
1 small red chilli, deseeded and chopped finely
250 g/8 oz/1 cup lean minced (ground) beef
1 tbsp fish sauce or mushroom ketchup
1 tbsp chopped fresh coriander (cilantro) or basil
2 tsp cornflour (cornstarch), blended with a little cold water
90 g/3 oz /¹⁄₂ cup cooked long-grain rice
salt and pepper

TO GARNISH:
sprigs of fresh coriander (cilantro) or basil
carrot slices

1 Slice the courgettes (zucchini) in half horizontally and scoop out a channel down the middle, discarding all the seeds. Sprinkle with salt and set aside for 15 minutes.

2 Heat the oil in a wok or frying pan (skillet) and add the garlic, shallots and chilli. Stir-fry for 2 minutes, until golden. Add the minced (ground) beef and stir-fry briskly for about 5 minutes.

Stir in the fish sauce or mushroom ketchup, the chopped coriander (cilantro) or basil and the blended cornflour (cornstarch), and cook for 2 minutes, stirring until thickened. Season with salt and pepper, then remove from the heat.

3 Rinse the courgettes (zucchini) in cold water and arrange them in a greased shallow ovenproof dish, cut side uppermost. Mix the cooked rice into the minced (ground) beef, then use this mixture to stuff the courgettes (zucchini).

4 Cover with foil and bake in a preheated oven at 190°C/375°F/ Gas Mark 5 for about 20–25 minutes, removing the foil for the last 5 minutes of cooking time. Serve at once, garnished with sprigs of fresh coriander (cilantro) or basil, and carrot slices.

VARIATIONS

Minced (ground) pork or chicken can be used instead of beef.

Vary the type of vegetables that you use. Aubergines (eggplants), large mushrooms and extra-large tomatoes all make good alternatives.

CHAPTER FIVE

Vegetable Dishes

In all Thai cookery, vegetables are used in abundance to add taste, colour and 'crunch' to an array of different dishes. They feature in many recipes for side dishes and stir-fries, in which they are cooked quickly to retain all their goodness and flavour. Quick cooking is one of the hallmarks of this country's vibrant cuisine, and Thai cooks take care to assemble all their ingredients before they start to cook, so that everything is to hand when things start to sizzle!

Obtaining fresh produce to use in Thai cookery shouldn't present a problem, as there is now such a wide range of fresh vegetables available, and it is easy to adapt and make substitutions that will work equally well. So while it may not always be possible to use the exact ingredient, dishes with a good degree of authenticity can still be achieved. For instance, where bok choy is used in the recipe for Stir-fried Greens, spring cabbage or spinach could be used instead.

Remember that in Thai cookery a few key ingredients can capture the flavour of the country. Coconut milk, fish sauce, fresh coriander (cilantro), lemon grass, Kaffir lime leaves and fresh chillies are all typical ingredients in many dishes from Thailand, and are all becoming more widely available.

Opposite: A stunning display of colourful and exotic ingredients in a Thai marketplace.

STEP 1

STEP 2

STEP 3

STEP 4

DEEP-FRIED VEGETABLES WITH SWEET & SOUR SAUCE

Choose a selection of your favourite seasonal vegetables, coat them in a light batter and deep-fry them until crispy to make this delightful dish.

SERVES 4

500 g/1 lb selection of fresh vegetables, such as red and green (bell) peppers, courgettes (zucchini), carrots, spring onions (scallions), cauliflower, broccoli and mushrooms
oil for deep-frying

BATTER:
125 g/4 oz/1 cup plain (all-purpose) flour
½ tsp salt
1 tsp caster (superfine) sugar
1 tsp baking powder
3 tbsp vegetable oil
200 ml/7 fl oz/scant 1 cup tepid water

SAUCE:
1 tbsp light muscovado sugar
2 tbsp soy sauce
4 tbsp cider vinegar
4 tbsp medium sherry
1 tbsp cornflour (cornstarch)
1 tsp finely grated fresh ginger root

TO GARNISH:
spring onion (scallion) brushes (see page 34)
chopped spring onions (scallions)

1 To make the batter, sift the flour, salt, sugar and baking powder into a large bowl. Add the oil and most of the water. Whisk together to make a smooth batter, adding extra water to give it the consistency of single (light) cream. Chill for 20–30 minutes.

2 To make the sauce, put all the ingredients into a small saucepan. Heat, stirring, until thickened and smooth.

3 Cut all the vegetables into even, bite-sized pieces.

4 Heat the oil in a wok or deep fat fryer. Dip the vegetables into the batter and fry them in the hot oil, a few at a time, until golden brown and crispy, about 2 minutes. Drain on paper towels.

5 Serve the vegetables on a warmed platter, garnished with spring onion (scallion) brushes and chopped spring onions (scallions), accompanied by the sauce.

SESAME SEEDS

Scatter a few sesame seeds over the crispy-fried vegetables just before serving, if you wish.

STEP 1

STEP 2

STEP 3

STEP 4

BAMBOO SHOOTS WITH CUCUMBER

A simple stir-fried side dish of canned bamboo shoots and sliced cucumber is the perfect accompaniment to a Thai main meal.

SERVES 4

¹/₂ cucumber
2 tbsp sesame oil
4 shallots, chopped finely
1 garlic clove, sliced finely
350 g/12 oz can of bamboo shoots, drained
1 tbsp dry sherry
1 tbsp soy sauce
2 tsp cornflour (cornstarch)
1 tsp sesame seeds
salt

TO GARNISH:
2 red chilli flowers
sliced spring onions (scallions)

1 Slice the cucumber thinly and sprinkle with salt. Leave for 10–15 minutes, then rinse with cold water. To make chilli flowers for garnishing, hold the stem of the chilli and cut down its length several times with a sharp knife. Place in a bowl of chilled water and chill so that the 'petals' turn out. Remove the chilli seeds when the 'petals' have opened.

2 Heat the sesame oil in a wok or frying pan (skillet) and add the shallots and garlic. Stir-fry for 2 minutes, until golden.

3 Add the bamboo shoots and cucumber to the wok or frying pan (skillet) and stir-fry for 2–3 minutes.

4 Blend together the sherry, soy sauce and cornflour (cornstarch). Add to the bamboo shoots and cucumber, stirring to combine. Cook for 1–2 minutes to thicken slightly, then add the sesame seeds and stir them through.

5 Transfer the vegetables to a warmed serving dish. Garnish with the chilli flowers and chopped spring onion (scallion). Serve at once.

TIPS

Salting the cucumber before it is stir-fried draws out some of its moisture so that it stays crisp.
   Add some very finely sliced carrot to this dish to add some extra colour, if you like.

STEP 1

STEP 2

STEP 3

STEP 4

STIR-FRIED GREENS

Eat your greens in this most delicious way – stir-fried so that they retain their colour, crunch and flavour.

SERVES 4

8 spring onions (scallions)
2 celery sticks
125 g/4 oz white radish (mooli)
125 g/4 oz sugar snap peas or mangetout (snow peas)
175 g/6 oz Chinese leaves or cabbage
175 g/6 oz bok choy or spinach
2 tbsp vegetable oil
1 tbsp sesame oil
2 garlic cloves, chopped finely
1 tbsp fish sauce
2 tbsp oyster sauce
1 tsp finely grated fresh ginger root
pepper

1 Slice the spring onions (scallions) and celery finely. Cut the white radish (mooli) into matchstick strips. Trim the sugar snap peas or mangetout (snow peas). Shred the Chinese leaves or cabbage and shred the bok choy or spinach.

2 Heat the vegetable oil and sesame oil together in a wok or large frying pan (skillet). Add the garlic and fry for about 1 minute.

3 Add the spring onions (scallions), celery, white radish (mooli) and sugar snap peas or mangetout (snow peas) to the wok or frying pan (skillet) and stir-fry for about 2 minutes.

4 Add the Chinese leaves or cabbage and bok choy or spinach. Stir-fry for 1 minute.

5 Stir the fish sauce and oyster sauce into the vegetables with the grated ginger. Cook for 1 minute. Season with pepper and serve at once.

VARIATIONS

Any variety – and any amount – of fresh vegetables can be used in this dish. Just make sure that harder vegetables, such as carrots, are cut very finely so that they cook quickly.

Use light soy sauce as an alternative to the fish sauce, if you prefer.

STEP 1

STEP 2

STEP 3

STEP 4

SHREDDED VEGETABLE OMELETTE

Cook this large omelette and then slice into four portions to serve as a side dish. If you like, double the quantities and serve it as a main course.

SERVES 4

4 eggs
3 tbsp milk
1 tbsp fish sauce or light soy sauce
1 tbsp sesame oil
1 small red onion, very finely sliced
1 small courgette (zucchini), trimmed and
   cut into matchstick pieces
1 small leek, trimmed and cut into
   matchstick pieces
1 small carrot, trimmed and cut into
   matchstick pieces
5 cm/2 inch piece of cucumber, cut into
   matchstick pieces
1 tbsp chopped fresh coriander (cilantro)
15 g/½ oz/1 tbsp butter
salt and pepper

TO GARNISH:
sprigs of fresh basil
celery leaves
4 chilli flowers (see page 68)

1 Beat the eggs, milk and fish sauce or soy sauce together.

2 Heat the sesame oil in a wok or large frying pan (skillet) and add all the vegetables. Stir-fry them briskly for 3–4 minutes, then add the chopped coriander (cilantro). Season with salt and

pepper. Transfer to a warmed plate and keep warm.

3 Melt the butter in a large omelette pan or frying pan (skillet) and add the beaten egg mixture. Cook over a medium-high heat until just set.

4 Tip the vegetable mixture along one side of the omelette, then roll up the omelette. Slice into 4 portions and arrange on a warmed serving plate. Garnish with fresh basil, celery leaves and chilli flowers and serve at once.

VEGETABLES

Work quickly when making the omelette to make sure that the vegetables retain their just-cooked texture and flavour.

Substitute other vegetables for the ones in the recipe as you wish – spring onions (scallions), mangetout (snow peas), small broccoli or cauliflower florets, for example.

STEP 1

STEP 2

STEP 3

STEP 4

PAW-PAW (PAPAYA) SALAD

Choose firm paw-paws – or papayas as they are sometimes called – for this delicious salad.

SERVES 4

DRESSING:
4 tbsp olive oil
1 tbsp fish sauce or light soy sauce
2 tbsp lime or lemon juice
1 tbsp dark muscovado sugar
1 tsp finely chopped fresh red or green chilli

SALAD:
1 crisp lettuce
¼ small white cabbage
2 paw-paws (papayas)
2 tomatoes
30 g/1 oz/¼ cup roast peanuts, chopped roughly
4 spring onions (scallions), trimmed and sliced thinly
basil leaves, to garnish

1 To make the dressing, whisk together the olive oil, fish sauce or soy sauce, lime or lemon juice, sugar and chopped chilli. Set aside, stirring occasionally to dissolve the sugar.

2 Shred the lettuce and cabbage and toss them together. Arrange on a large serving plate.

3 Peel the paw-paws (papayas) and slice them in half. Scoop out the seeds, then slice the flesh thinly. Arrange on top of the shredded lettuce and cabbage.

4 Put the tomatoes into a small bowl and cover them with boiling water. Leave them to stand for 1 minute, then lift them out with a fork and peel them. Remove the seeds and chop the flesh. Arrange them on the salad leaves. Scatter the peanuts and spring onions (scallions) over the top.

5 Whisk the salad dressing to distribute the ingredients and pour over the salad. Garnish with basil leaves and serve at once.

TIPS

Instead of using a fresh chilli in the dressing, use ½ teaspoon of dried chilli flakes instead. If you prefer a milder dressing, omit the chilli altogether.

Choose plain, unsalted peanuts and toast them under the grill (broiler) until golden to get the best flavour. Take care not to burn them, as they brown very quickly.

THAI COOKING

INGREDIENTS
Keep a wide selection of Thai ingredients in your kitchen store cupboard (cabinet): cans of coconut milk, creamed coconut, chilli sauces, plum sauce, fish sauce, soy sauce and a selection of rice and noodles. Many of these things will keep for some time, and will make an impromptu Thai meal much easier to tackle.

Fresh ingredients
Buy fresh ingredients as and when you need them. The flavour of any recipe is only as good as the ingredients. Coriander (cilantro), garlic, Kaffir lime leaves, chillies and vegetables are all best when used fresh. These are best bought in small quantities, so that they are more affordable, and are not wasted if left unused for too long in the refrigerator.

Advance preparation
When making any Thai recipe, the cooking method is generally very quick, so it is an excellent idea to prepare all your ingredients first, so they are ready when you need them.

Curry paste
Red and green Thai curry pastes can be bought at most supermarkets, so make sure that you have at least one jar of each. Store them in the refrigerator after opening and check the storage times.

Welcome to the world of Thai cookery – a cuisine full of colour, flavour and sheer vibrancy, where the natural good taste of the most delicious ingredients comes bursting through, right on to your serving plate!

Thai cookery is a very healthy cuisine, where masses of fresh vegetables, fish and seafood combine with rice and noodles to give extremely well-balanced meals. Meat and poultry feature too, though not in the same quantities as fish. This is easy to appreciate when you remember that Thailand is a country surrounded by thousands of miles of coastline, with many inland rivers and waterways too, making fish and seafood one of the country's most plentiful resources.

The cuisine of this colourful country is quick to prepare and cook – a valuable asset these days, as everyone's time is precious, often with little available for spending in the kitchen. It is reassuring, too, to know that mastering the art of another country's culinary techniques need not take a lifetime. In fact, the basics of Thai cookery can be absorbed very quickly. Let this step-by-step guide to Thai side dishes lead you through some of the most interesting recipes that Thailand has to offer.

INGREDIENTS
The first question you are sure to ask when trying out a new type of cookery is, 'Will I be able to get all the ingredients that I need?' The answer is yes – provided you know where to look. It is surprising just how much variety and choice is now available, and if you can't find what you are looking for – ask! By creating a demand for a particular ingredient, you may persuade the manager of the store to stock it. If you can't find certain ingredients in a supermarket, it is often worth asking if they are stocked, as they are often there, but not necessarily where you expect to find them.

So just which ingredients are most often used in Thai cookery? The following list summarizes the most important foods and flavourings added to many different dishes to give them their distinctive characteristics.

Chillies
Chillies add heat and flavour to Thai recipes and are inextricably linked to the cuisine of the country. They are sold as red, green and yellow, and the general rule is 'the smaller the chillies, the hotter they are'! So if you wish to become accustomed to Thai food gradually, start with a small quantity of fresh chilli, choose the larger varieties in preference to the smaller ones and remove all the seeds. When your tastebuds adapt, you can progress to smaller chillies, and more of them!

Be very careful when preparing fresh chillies, as the juices can burn and irritate the skin. Make sure that you never rub your eyes during their preparation, and do wash your hands and scrub your nails thoroughly afterwards, to ensure that all traces are removed. To be on the safe side, you can wear thin rubber gloves when you prepare them.

You can often substitute dried chillies for fresh ones, or you can use chilli powder instead. Let your own tastes guide you, and if you really don't like the heat that chillies add to food, you can leave them out altogether. You could try using some red or green (bell) peppers instead, both within the recipe and for garnishing.

Chilli sauce

Numerous brands of chilli sauce are now available, so there should be plenty of different types to choose from. Some Thai food retailers also make up their own special versions, so look out for these. Sometimes the sauce is added to the recipe simply to create heat and flavour, and sometimes it is made up as a fresh, separate side dish for serving with food. For example, see the recipe for Prawns (Shrimp) with Hot & Sweet Dipping Sauce on page 22.

If you are unsure of your guests' preferences, it may be safer to serve a Thai meal with extra chilli sauce at the table, so that your guests can season their food. Some may like it hot, but others may have their meal spoiled if it is too hot for them to enjoy.

Coconut milk

Coconut milk can cause confusion in culinary terms, as it is *not* the liquid found inside coconuts! It is the liquid produced when the white flesh of the coconut is grated or shredded, soaked in water or milk, then squeezed to extract all the flavour. It is this that adds a delicious flavour and creaminess to many Thai recipes.

While you can make your own coconut milk from fresh coconuts, you can now also buy cans of coconut milk very easily, or look out for creamed coconut in packets, which can be mixed with warm water or milk before being added to your recipes.

Sometimes you may see references to coconut 'cream'. This is the first extraction of liquid after soaking the grated fresh coconut flesh in water or milk. Second, or even third extractions can be made by repeating the process of soaking the coconut flesh in fresh water or milk, to give a liquid with a thinner consistency and less pronounced flavour. Another way to make coconut milk is to soak unsweetened desiccated (shredded) coconut in tepid milk or water, then squeeze out the liquid as before.

Make sure that you use coconut milk within two days of making it, and store it in the refrigerator in an airtight container. If you are using a can and there is some left, pour it into a plastic storage box and chill it for up to 2 days. Unused coconut milk can also be frozen if preferred, though remember to use it within 2 months.

Coriander (cilantro)

This wonderful herb has a very distinctive flavour, appreciated throughout Thailand and extensively used in Thai cookery. It is from the parsley family, and looks quite similar to flat-leafed varieties, but it does not

Seafood

Keep some seafood in the freezer, ready for use in Thai meals. Frozen prawns (shrimp) and squid all come in handy, and keep well if frozen. However, make sure you mark the freezer container with the date, to make sure they don't stay in there too long. It is also very useful to keep some cans of fish too.

Spices

Measure out all the spices that you need before you start to cook, and put them on a plate in the order they are required. Spices should be kept in a cool, dark, dry cupboard to preserve their freshness, and used up quickly. It can be helpful to mark the jar or packet with the date on which you bought it, to prevent it from sitting on the shelf for months on end!

UTENSILS

Utensils for Thai cookery are quite basic – you don't need any expensive equipment.

Woks

A wok is important for the stir-frying that you will be doing, and it can also be used for deep-frying. Some come with a trellis that will enable you to steam food in the wok, so look around for the most adaptable type if you are going to buy a new one. They often come with some basic utensils, such as a rice paddle, chopsticks and maybe even a metal spatula.

Pestle and mortar

If you don't already own one, a mortar and pestle is a good investment for grinding spices and herbs and making your own curry pastes.

Choose a large, deep mortar so that there is plenty of room to pound the ingredients together. Thai ones are made from earthenware, so buy one of those if you can. They are designed to cope with moist curry pastes, and they are generally less expensive than other types. As there is a bit of friction from the rough surface, many cooks find them more efficient than the smooth marble-type that can also be bought.

Steamer

A steamer is a good investment. Buy one that fits over different sizes of saucepan so that you can make meals for one or for a crowd equally easily. Make sure also that the lid fits tightly.

Alternatively, you can just buy one of the inexpensive folding metal steamers that fit inside saucepans, which have their own short legs to keep them off the base of the saucepan and above the water.

Bamboo baskets are ideal for steaming. They are usually cheap to buy, and they look so attractive that they can be taken straight to the dinner table, which will delight your guests, and save on the washing-up.

emulate parsley in flavour, so the two cannot be interchanged.

In Thai cooking, coriander (cilantro) plants are very effective and economical, as the whole plant can be used. The roots can be scrubbed and finely ground or chopped for use in curry pastes, the stems and leaves are used in soups and stews, and the leaves are used in salads and for garnishing. Wherever the herb is used, it adds its fresh, strong, distinctive flavour to the dish.

Fresh coriander (cilantro) can be bought from many supermarkets, where you will find it either in individual packs or in growing pots. If you can manage to buy coriander (cilantro) plants with the roots still on, keep them in water; otherwise keep cut coriander (cilantro) chilled in a plastic bag.

Coriander seed is also used in Thai cookery, though not as frequently as the fresh herb. Its use is more restricted to the making of curry pastes.

Fish sauce (Nam pla)

Fish sauce is widely used throughout Thailand as a seasoning sauce, in much the same way as soy sauce is used, and the two are often used together. While the flavour of fish sauce by itself is very pungent, it adds subtlety and character to the finished dish when used in small quantities with lots of other ingredients, so do not be put off by the flavour of fish sauce alone!

The sauce is thin, clear and salty, and can be light to dark brown in colour. Because it is salty, it often means that salt itself is unnecessary in Thai recipes where fish sauce is used, so go carefully

and always taste the food before adding extra salt.

Fish sauce is made by layering fish and salt in large barrels, which are then left for 3 to 4 months to ferment. The resulting liquid is then siphoned off, filtered and bottled, ready to use in numerous Thai recipes.

Galangal

Resembling fresh ginger root in appearance, galangal has a pale yellow colour with pink shoots. It is also known as 'Laos' or Thai ginger. The root is not used alone, but is ground and combined with other ingredients to make the base flavouring for the red and green Thai curry pastes, or added to soups and steamed dishes.

Fresh galangal can be bought from Thai food stockists, and sometimes forms one of the ingredients in packs of fresh Thai herbs and flavourings. Dried galangal is also available – look for it on the spice racks in supermarkets. This will need to be soaked before use, so read the label first to check the instructions.

Garlic

Garlic is widely used in Thai cookery, adding its flavour and pungency to a great many dishes. It is also served in Thailand as pickled garlic, a popular snack or side dish, where whole garlic cloves are preserved in a sweet or acidic vinegar. In Thailand the garlic bulbs tend to be smaller than ones sold in the UK and US, and the cloves are not peeled before use. Peeling the cloves is recommended unless they are very young and tender.

Kaffir lime leaves

In the same way that bay leaves are added to soups and stews in European cooking, Kaffir lime leaves are added to Thai recipes to impart their distinctive lime-like flavour. They are dark green, shiny and leathery, and have a kind of double-leaf appearance.

You may find Kaffir lime leaves in the small packs of fresh Thai herbs and flavourings that are sold in many supermarkets. If you have difficulty finding them, substitute the pared rind of a lime.

Lemon grass

This aromatic plant with its distinctive fragrance and lemon flavour has been used for centuries, both as a medicinal herb and for its culinary flavour. It is known as citronella in Europe, and its many uses have ranged from an insect-repellent to a calming tea for Buddhist monks.

Now widely available in supermarkets and some greengrocers, fresh lemon grass forms an important flavour-base to many Thai dishes, and particularly to soups and stews. In cookery, the stalk of the lemon grass plant is used, where it needs to be washed, then bruised or slit open lengthways so that the full flavour is released. The easiest way to bruise a piece of lemon grass is to bash it all over with a rolling pin, a pestle or a meat mallet.

The stalk of the lemon grass imparts its wonderful flavour to the cooking liquid, then it is removed and discarded before the dish is served. Alternatively, it can be chopped or finely sliced.

Store fresh lemon grass in the refrigerator, wrapped loosely in clingfilm (plastic wrap) or in a brown paper bag.

Dried chopped lemon grass can be bought too, and while it does not have the same intensity of flavour as fresh, it is a useful store cupboard standby. Remember that dried lemon grass needs to be soaked in a little tepid water before use. You can find this product among the herbs and spices in your local supermarket.

As a substitute for either fresh or dried lemon grass, finely grated lemon rind could be used instead, although the finished dish will not have quite the same flavour.

Limes

Limes feature frequently in Thai cookery, for flavouring and garnishing. They are used in preference to lemons because they have a more acidic flavour, which adds a freshness and sharpness to many recipes. Lemons can be used instead, if you cannot find limes.

Sesame oil

Sesame oil is made from sesame seeds and has a deliciously nutty flavour, making it an ideal choice for stir-fries, where its distinctive taste complements the other ingredients. Because of its pronounced flavour, its use is best reserved for recipes where only small quantities are needed, otherwise it could be overpowering. It is also more expensive than other oils, so should be made to last. Do not use it for deep-frying, as it will burn before it reaches the correct temperature.

Knives

Keep your knives sharpened! So much of Thai cookery involves cutting and slicing food into small pieces that it is very important to do it quickly, efficiently and safely. A good cook's knife is an important tool, yet it is surprising how few people possess them or use them correctly. Watch a chef at work and you will soon see how he uses his knife! Make sure that you have some good, large chopping (cutting) boards too, so that your work surfaces (counters) are protected. A tiny paring knife is useful for carving decorative garnishes from fruit and vegetables, which is a characteristic of Thai cooking, and can be very enjoyable to do.

GARNISHES

Practise the art of garnishing food attractively, as it is often the finishing touches that make all the difference. Prepare your garnishes before you start to cook, in readiness for the finished food. After all, when you have gone to the trouble of cooking something new and exciting, you may as well make it a feast for the eyes too! Many garnishes, such as cucumber leaves and chilli flowers, are explained in the recipes in this book, but experiment with your own. It can be an entertaining way to pass the time, while you are waiting for something to finish cooking!

INDEX